CSS

TYPOGRAPHY

and Web Fonts

Abdelfattah Ragab

CSS Typography and Web Fonts

Abdelfattah Ragab

Introduction

Welcome to the book "CSS Typography and Web Fonts".

In this book I will explain the CSS typography properties that control font sizes, line heights, letter spacing and so on.

By the end of this book, you will be able to insert your custom fonts into your web applications, change the font properties and handle all kinds of scenarios.

Let us go!

Chapter 1: Font-related properties

font-family

The font-family property defines the font for an element. The font-family property can contain several font names as a "fallback" system. If the browser does not support the first font, it tries the next font.

There are two types of font family names:

- family-name - The name of a font family, such as "times", "courier", "arial", etc.
- generic-family - The name of a generic family, e.g. "serif", "sans-serif", "cursive", "fantasy", "monospace".

Start with the desired font and always end with a generic family so that the browser can select a similar font from the generic family if no other fonts are available.

Separate the individual values with a comma.

If the name of a font contains spaces, it must be enclosed in quotation marks as follows:

```
font-family: "Times New Roman", serif;
```

Values

- family-name, .., generic-family

family-name, .., generic-family

Lorem ipsum dolor sit amet consectetur adipisicing elit. Minus magni alias odit quia optio quae eaque, sed enim a laboriosam numquam neque velit qui maiores quos nostrum facere in ab. Reiciendis, nostrum obcaecati dolore vel nam quidem molestias eos magnam quibusdam aliquid accusamus sed nesciunt necessitatibus commodi voluptatum similique et!

```
<style>
  p {
    font-size: 30px;
    font-family: Arial, Helvetica, sans-serif;
  }
</style>
<p>
  Lorem ipsum dolor sit amet consectetur
adipisicing elit. Minus magni alias
  odit quia optio quae eaque, sed enim a
laboriosam numquam neque velit qui
  maiores quos nostrum facere in ab.
Reiciendis, nostrum obcaecati dolore vel
  nam quidem molestias eos magnam quibusdam
aliquid accusamus sed nesciunt
```

necessitatibus commodi voluptatum similique et!

</p>

```html
1  <style>
2    p {
3      font-size: 30px;
4      font-family: Arial, Helvetica, sans-serif;
5    }
6  </style>
7  <p>
8    Lorem ipsum dolor sit amet consectetur adipisicing elit. Minus magni alias
9    odit quia optio quae eaque, sed enim a laboriosam numquam neque velit qui
10   maiores quos nostrum facere in ab. Reiciendis, nostrum obcaecati dolore vel
11   nam quidem molestias eos magnam quibusdam aliquid accusamus sed nesciunt
12   necessitatibus commodi voluptatum similique et!
13 </p>
```

font-size

The font-size property sets the size of a font.

Values

- keyword
- length
- %

Keywords

- medium (default)
- xx-small
- x-small
- small
- large
- x-large
- xx-large
- smaller
- larger

medium (default)

Set the font size to a medium size.

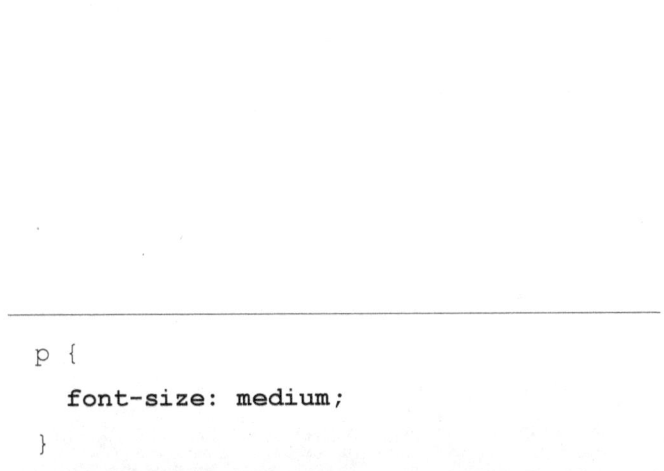

```css
p {

    font-size: medium;

}
```

length

Sets the font-size to a fixed size in px, cm, etc.

```css
p {
    font-size: 30px;
}
```

```
2  p {
3      font-size: 30px;
4  }
```

%

Sets the font-size to a percent of the parent element's font size.

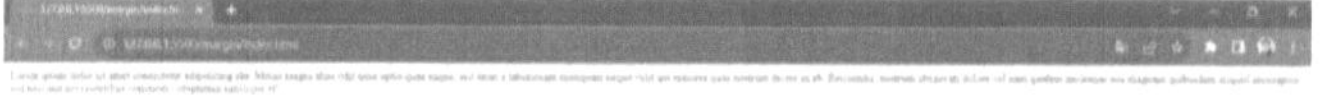

```css
p {
   font-size: 80%;
}
```

```
2  p {
3     font-size: 80%;
4  }
```

font-weight

The font-weight CSS property sets the weight (or boldness) of the font. The weights available depend on the font-family that is currently set.

Values

- keyword
- numeric values [1,1000]

Keywords

- normal (default)
- bold
- bolder
- lighter

Numeric values

- 100
- 200
- 300
- 400 normal
- 500

- 600
- 700 bold
- 800
- 900

Normal font weight. Same as 400.

Lorem ipsum dolor sit amet consectetur adipisicing elit. Minus magni alias odit quia optio quae eaque, sed enim a laboriosam numquam neque velit qui maiores quos nostrum facere in ab. Reiciendis, nostrum obcaecati dolore vel nam quidem molestias eos magnam quibusdam aliquid accusamus sed nesciunt necessitatibus commodi voluptatum similique et!

```
p {

    font-size: 30px;

    font-weight: normal;

}
```

```
2  p {
3      font-size: 30px;
4      font-weight: normal;
5  }
```


Bold font weight. Same as 700.

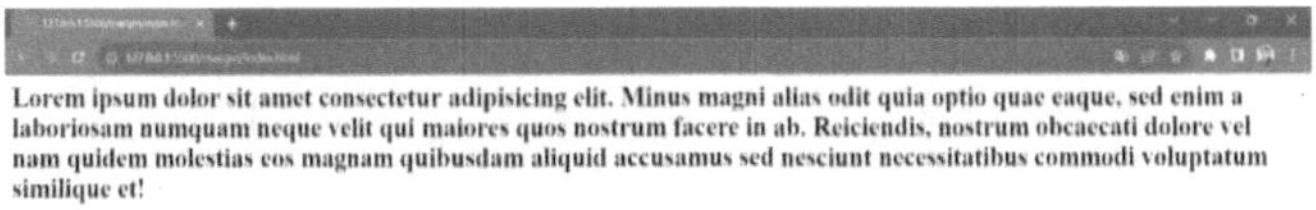

Lorem ipsum dolor sit amet consectetur adipisicing elit. Minus magni alias odit quia optio quae eaque, sed enim a laboriosam numquam neque velit qui maiores quos nostrum facere in ab. Reiciendis, nostrum obcaecati dolore vel nam quidem molestias eos magnam quibusdam aliquid accusamus sed nesciunt necessitatibus commodi voluptatum similique et!

```css
p {
    font-size: 30px;
    font-weight: bold;
}
```

```
2  p {
3      font-size: 30px;
4      font-weight: bold;
5  }
```

numeric value

100 to 900 defines thin to thick letters. 400 stands for normal and 700 for bold.

Lorem ipsum dolor sit amet consectetur adipisicing elit. Minus magni alias odit quia optio quae eaque, sed enim a laboriosam numquam neque velit qui maiores quos nostrum facere in ab. Reiciendis, nostrum obcaecati dolore vel nam quidem molestias eos magnam quibusdam aliquid accusamus sed nesciunt necessitatibus commodi voluptatum similique et!

```css
p {
    font-size: 30px;
    font-weight: 700;
}
```

```css
2  p {
3      font-size: 30px;
4      font-weight: 700;
5  }
```

font-style

The font-style property specifies the font style for a text.

Values

- normal (default)
- italic
- oblique

normal (default)

The browser displays a normal font style.

Lorem ipsum dolor sit amet consectetur adipisicing elit. Minus magni alias odit quia optio quae eaque, sed enim a laboriosam numquam neque velit qui maiores quos nostrum facere in ab. Reiciendis, nostrum obcaecati dolore vel nam quidem molestias eos magnam quibusdam aliquid accusamus sed nesciunt necessitatibus commodi voluptatum similique et!

```css
p {
    font-size: 30px;
    font-style: normal;
}
```

```
2  p {
3    font-size: 30px;
4    font-style: normal;
5  }
```

italic

The browser displays an italic font style

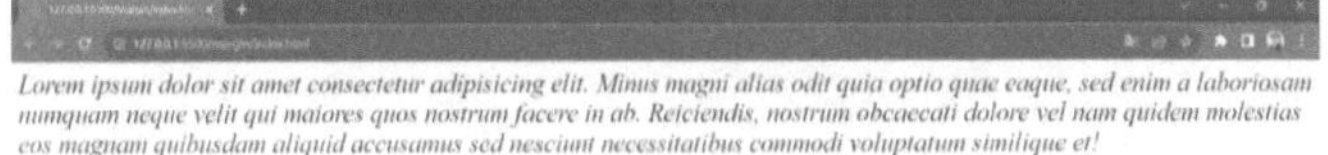

Lorem ipsum dolor sit amet consectetur adipisicing elit. Minus magni alias odit quia optio quae eaque, sed enim a laboriosam numquam neque velit qui maiores quos nostrum facere in ab. Reiciendis, nostrum obcaecati dolore vel nam quidem molestias eos magnam quibusdam aliquid accusamus sed nesciunt necessitatibus commodi voluptatum similique et!

```css
p {
  font-size: 30px;
  font-style: italic;
}
```

```css
p {
  font-size: 30px;
  font-style: italic;
}
```

oblique

The browser displays an oblique font style

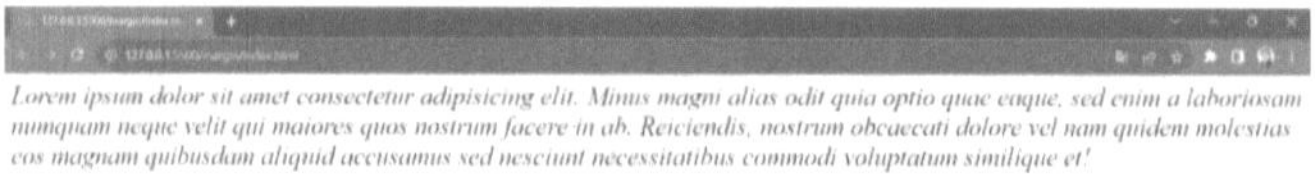

Lorem ipsum dolor sit amet consectetur adipisicing elit. Minus magni alias odit quia optio quae eaque, sed enim a laboriosam numquam neque velit qui maiores quos nostrum facere in ab. Reiciendis, nostrum obcaecati dolore vel nam quidem molestias eos magnam quibusdam aliquid accusamus sed nesciunt necessitatibus commodi voluptatum similique et!

```css
p {
  font-size: 30px;
  font-style: oblique;
}
```

```css
p {
  font-size: 30px;
  font-style: oblique;
}
```

Italic vs oblique

Italic and oblique are two different styles used in typography to emphasize or alter the appearance of text. While they have similar visual effects, there are some key differences between them.

Italic

Italic is a style that originated from calligraphy and is designed to simulate the appearance of handwriting. Italic typefaces are created with a slight slant or lean to the right, with letters often having cursive or flowing characteristics. Italic typefaces are typically designed as separate fonts and have distinct letterforms that differ from the regular or roman typefaces. Italic fonts are used for emphasis, to indicate book titles, foreign words, or for differentiating quoted text within a paragraph. They are considered more versatile and aesthetically pleasing for extended reading than oblique typefaces.

Oblique

Oblique is a style that is created by artificially slanting the regular or roman typeface without making any other changes to the letterforms. Unlike italic, oblique typefaces are not designed as separate fonts but are simply a slanted version of the regular typeface. The slant is typically achieved by skewing the vertical axis of the characters. As a result, oblique typefaces maintain the same letterforms as the regular typeface but appear slanted. Oblique fonts are often used as a substitute for italic when an italic typeface is not available for a particular font family. However, they lack the same aesthetic qualities as true italic fonts.

@font-face

The CSS @font-face rule specifies a custom font to be used to display the text; the font can be loaded either from a remote server or from a font installed locally on your own computer.

Descriptors

- font-family
- src
- font-stretch
- font-style
- font-weight
- unicode-range

Example

Lorem ipsum dolor sit amet consectetur adipisicing elit. Aspernatur rem quae soluta nam aliquid assumenda dolorum. Dignissimos incidunt beatae illo adipisci vitae exercitationem ad, dicta, quasi optio suscipit minima autem reprehenderit provident? Ducimus quod doloribus eligendi vero id mollitia animi repudiandae reiciendis voluptate? Non minima, id dignissimos at ipsum quidem.

```css
<style>
  @font-face {
    font-family: "Feelfree";
    src:
url("FeelfreePersonalUseRegular-lg2Bw.ttf");
    font-stretch: normal;
    font-style: normal;
    font-weight: normal;
    unicode-range: U+00-7F;
  }
  p {
    font-size: 70px;
    padding: 80px;
    color: blue;
    font-family: "Feelfree";
  }
```

</style>

<p>

Lorem ipsum dolor sit amet consectetur adipisicing elit. Aspernatur rem quae soluta nam aliquid assumenda dolorum. Dignissimos incidunt beatae illo adipisci vitae exercitationem ad, dicta, quasi optio suscipit minima autem reprehenderit provident? Ducimus quod doloribus eligendi vero id mollitia animi repudiandae reiciendis voluptate? Non minima, id dignissimos at ipsum quidem.

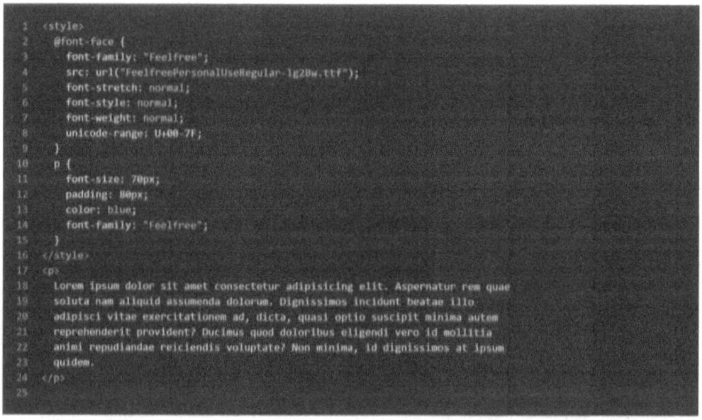

</p>

```html
1   <style>
2     @font-face {
3       font-family: "Feelfree";
4       src: url("FeelfreePersonalUseRegular-1g2Bw.ttf");
5       font-stretch: normal;
6       font-style: normal;
7       font-weight: normal;
8       unicode-range: U+00-7F;
9     }
10    p {
11      font-size: 70px;
12      padding: 80px;
13      color: blue;
14      font-family: "Feelfree";
15    }
16  </style>
17  <p>
18    Lorem ipsum dolor sit amet consectetur adipisicing elit. Aspernatur rem quae
19    soluta nam aliquid assumenda dolorum. Dignissimos incidunt beatae illo
20    adipisci vitae exercitationem ad, dicta, quasi optio suscipit minima autem
21    reprehenderit provident? Ducimus quod doloribus eligendi vero id mollitia
22    animi repudiandae reiciendis voluptate? Non minima, id dignissimos at ipsum
23    quidem.
24  </p>
25
```

Chapter 2: Text layout properties

line-height

The CSS property line-height defines the height of a line frame. It's often used to set the spacing between lines of text.

Values

- normal (default)
- number
- length
- %

normal (default)

A normal line height.

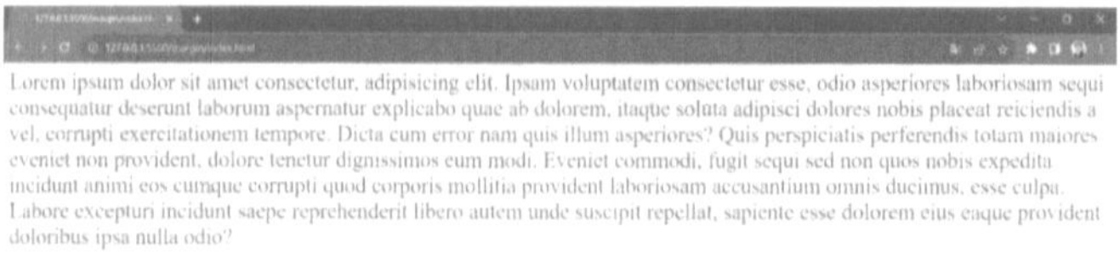

Lorem ipsum dolor sit amet consectetur, adipisicing elit. Ipsam voluptatem consectetur esse, odio asperiores laboriosam sequi consequatur deserunt laborum aspernatur explicabo quae ab dolorem, itaque soluta adipisci dolores nobis placeat reiciendis a vel, corrupti exercitationem tempore. Dicta cum error nam quis illum asperiores? Quis perspiciatis perferendis totam maiores eveniet non provident, dolore tenetur dignissimos eum modi. Eveniet commodi, fugit sequi sed non quos nobis expedita incidunt animi eos cumque corrupti quod corporis mollitia provident laboriosam accusantium omnis ducimus, esse culpa. Labore excepturi incidunt saepe reprehenderit libero autem unde suscipit repellat, sapiente esse dolorem eius eaque provident doloribus ipsa nulla odio?

```
<style>
  p {
    font-size: 30px;
    color: blue;
    line-height: normal;
  }
</style>
<p>
  Lorem ipsum dolor sit amet consectetur,
adipisicing elit. Ipsam voluptatem
  consectetur esse, odio asperiores laboriosam
sequi consequatur deserunt
  laborum aspernatur explicabo quae ab dolorem,
itaque soluta adipisci dolores
  nobis placeat reiciendis a vel, corrupti
exercitationem tempore. Dicta cum
```

error nam quis illum asperiores? Quis
perspiciatis perferendis totam maiores
    eveniet non provident, dolore tenetur
dignissimos eum modi. Eveniet commodi,
    fugit sequi sed non quos nobis expedita
incidunt animi eos cumque corrupti
    quod corporis mollitia provident laboriosam
accusantium omnis ducimus, esse
    culpa. Labore excepturi incidunt saepe
reprehenderit libero autem unde
    suscipit repellat, sapiente esse dolorem eius
eaque provident doloribus ipsa
    nulla odio?
</p>

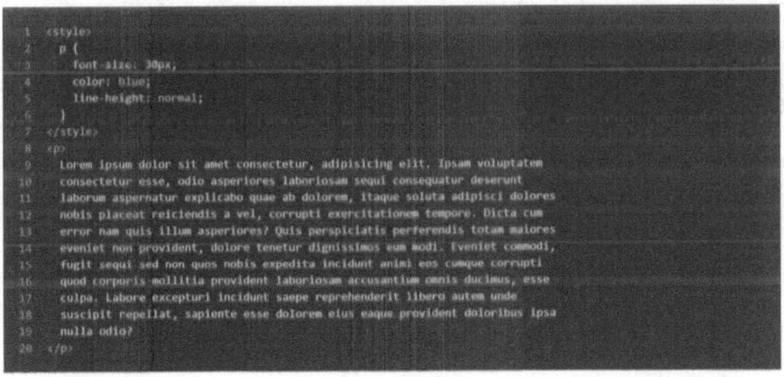

```
1   <style>
2     p {
3       font-size: 30px;
4       color: blue;
5       line-height: normal;
6     }
7   </style>
8   <p>
9     Lorem ipsum dolor sit amet consectetur, adipisicing elit. Ipsam voluptatem
10    consectetur esse, odio asperiores laboriosam sequi consequatur deserunt
11    laborum aspernatur explicabo quae ab dolorem, itaque soluta adipisci dolores
12    nobis placeat reiciendis a vel, corrupti exercitationem tempore. Dicta cum
13    error nam quis illum asperiores? Quis perspiciatis perferendis totam maiores
14    eveniet non provident, dolore tenetur dignissimos eum modi. Eveniet commodi,
15    fugit sequi sed non quos nobis expedita incidunt animi eos cumque corrupti
16    quod corporis mollitia provident laboriosam accusantium omnis ducimus, esse
17    culpa. Labore excepturi incidunt saepe reprehenderit libero autem unde
18    suscipit repellat, sapiente esse dolorem eius eaque provident doloribus ipsa
19    nulla odio?
20  </p>
```

number

A number that will be multiplied with the current font-size
to set the line height.

```css
p {
    font-size: 30px;
    color: blue;
    line-height: 2;
}
```

```
2  p {
3    font-size: 30px;
4    color: blue;
5    line-height: 2;
6  }
```

length

A fixed line height in px, pt, cm, etc.

Lorem ipsum dolor sit amet consectetur, adipisicing elit. Ipsam voluptatem consectetur esse, odio asperiores laboriosam sequi consequatur deserunt laborum aspernatur explicabo quae ab dolorem, itaque soluta adipisci dolores nobis placeat reiciendis a vel, corrupti exercitationem tempore. Dicta cum error nam quis illum asperiores? Quis perspiciatis perferendis totam maiores eveniet non provident, dolore tenetur dignissimos eum modi. Eveniet commodi, fugit sequi sed non quos nobis expedita incidunt animi eos cumque corrupti quod corporis mollitia provident laboriosam accusantium omnis ducimus, esse culpa. Labore excepturi incidunt saepe reprehenderit libero autem unde suscipit repellat, sapiente esse dolorem eius eaque provident doloribus ipsa nulla odio?

```css
p {
  font-size: 30px;
  color: blue;
  line-height: 80px;
}
```

```css
2  p {
3    font-size: 30px;
4    color: blue;
5    line-height: 80px;
6  }
```

%

A line height in percent of the current font size.

Lorem ipsum dolor sit amet consectetur, adipisicing elit. Ipsam voluptatem consectetur esse, odio asperiores laboriosam sequi consequatur deserunt laborum aspernatur explicabo quae ab dolorem, itaque soluta adipisci dolores nobis placeat reiciendis a vel, corrupti exercitationem tempore. Dicta cum error nam quis illum asperiores? Quis perspiciatis perferendis totam maiores eveniet non provident, dolore tenetur dignissimos eum modi. Eveniet commodi, fugit sequi sed non quos nobis expedita incidunt animi eos cumque corrupti quod corporis mollitia provident laboriosam accusantium omnis ducimus, esse culpa. Labore excepturi incidunt saepe reprehenderit libero autem unde suscipit repellat, sapiente esse dolorem eius eaque provident doloribus ipsa nulla odio?

```css
p {
    font-size: 30px;
    color: blue;
    line-height: 200%;
}
```

```css
2  p {
3      font-size: 30px;
4      color: blue;
5      line-height: 200%;
6  }
```

text-indent

The text-indent property defines the indentation of the first line in a text block.

Values

- length
- %

length

Defines a fixed indentation in px, pt, cm, em, etc. Default value is 0.

Lorem ipsum dolor sit amet consectetur, adipisicing elit. Ipsam voluptatem consectetur esse, odio asperiores laboriosam sequi consequatur deserunt laborum aspernatur explicabo quae ab dolorem, itaque soluta adipisci dolores nobis placeat reiciendis a vel, corrupti exercitationem tempore. Dicta cum error nam quis illum asperiores? Quis perspiciatis perferendis totam maiores eveniet non provident, dolore tenetur dignissimos eum modi. Eveniet commodi, fugit sequi sed non quos nobis expedita incidunt animi eos cumque corrupti quod corporis mollitia provident laboriosam accusantium omnis ducimus, esse culpa. Labore excepturi incidunt saepe reprehenderit libero autem unde suscipit repellat, sapiente esse dolorem eius eaque provident doloribus ipsa nulla odio?

```
<style>
  p {
    font-size: 30px;
    color: blue;
    line-height: 1.6;
    text-indent: 60px;
  }
</style>
<p>
  Lorem ipsum dolor sit amet consectetur,
adipisicing elit. Ipsam voluptatem
  consectetur esse, odio asperiores laboriosam
sequi consequatur deserunt
```

laborum aspernatur explicabo quae ab dolorem, itaque soluta adipisci dolores

nobis placeat reiciendis a vel, corrupti exercitationem tempore.

```
</p>
```

```
1   <style>
2     p {
3       font-size: 30px;
4       color: blue;
5       line-height: 1.6;
6       text-indent: 60px;
7     }
8   </style>
9   <p>
10    Lorem ipsum dolor sit amet consectetur, adipisicing elit. Ipsam voluptatem
11    consectetur esse, odio asperiores laboriosam sequi consequatur deserunt
12    laborum aspernatur explicabo quae ab dolorem, itaque soluta adipisci dolores
13    nobis placeat reiciendis a vel, corrupti exercitationem tempore.
14  </p>
```

%

Defines the indentation in % of the width of the parent element.

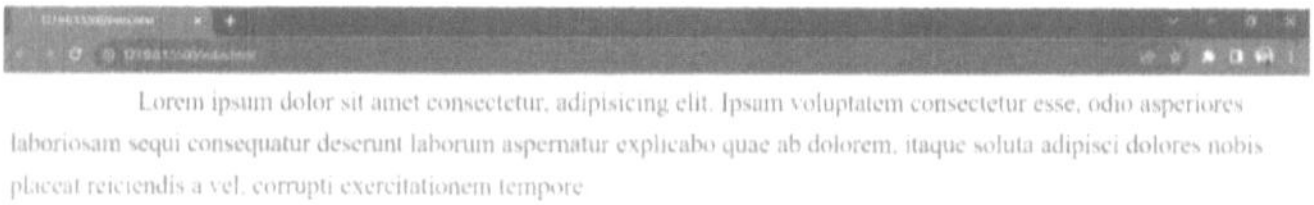

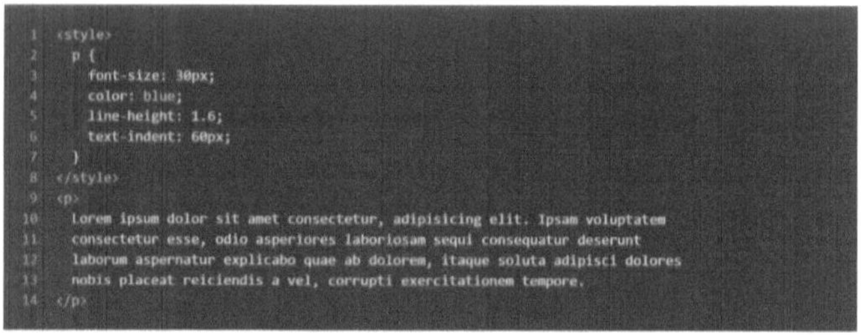

```
p {
    font-size: 30px;
    color: blue;
```

```css
line-height: 1.6;
text-indent: 10%;
}
```

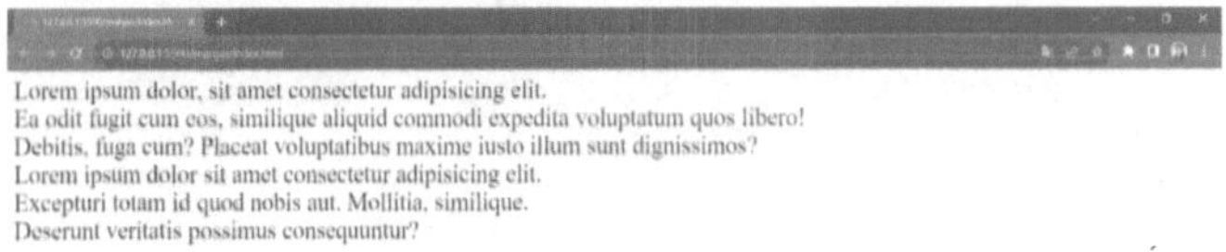

text-align

The text-align property specifies the horizontal alignment of text in an element.

Values

- left
- right
- center
- justify

left

Aligns the text to the left.

```html
<style>
  p {
    font-size: 30px;
    text-align: left;
  }
</style>
<p>
  Lorem ipsum dolor, sit amet consectetur
adipisicing elit.
  <br />
  Ea odit fugit cum eos, similique aliquid
commodi expedita voluptatum quos
  libero!
  <br />
  Debitis, fuga cum? Placeat voluptatibus
maxime iusto illum sunt dignissimos?
  <br />
  Lorem ipsum dolor sit amet consectetur
adipisicing elit.
  <br />
  Excepturi totam id quod nobis aut. Mollitia,
similique.
  <br />
  Deserunt veritatis possimus consequuntur?
</p>
```

```
<style>
  p {
    font-size: 30px;
    text-align: left;
  }
</style>
<p>
  Lorem ipsum dolor, sit amet consectetur adipisicing elit.
  <br />
  Ea odit fugit cum eos, similique aliquid commodi expedita voluptatum quos
  libero!
  <br />
  Debitis, fuga cum? Placeat voluptatibus maxime iusto illum sunt dignissimos?
  <br />
  Lorem ipsum dolor sit amet consectetur adipisicing elit.
  <br />
  Excepturi totam id quod nobis aut. Mollitia, similique.
  <br />
  Deserunt veritatis possimus consequuntur?
</p>
```

right

Aligns the text to the right.

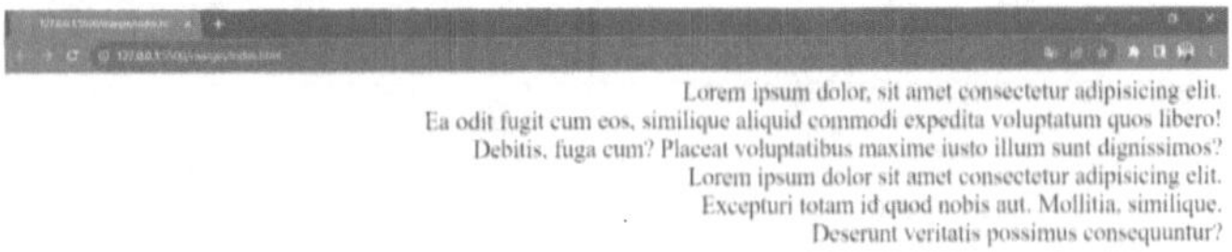

```
p {

  font-size: 30px;

  text-align: right;

}
```

```
p {
  font-size: 30px;
  text-align: right;
}
```

center

Centers the text.

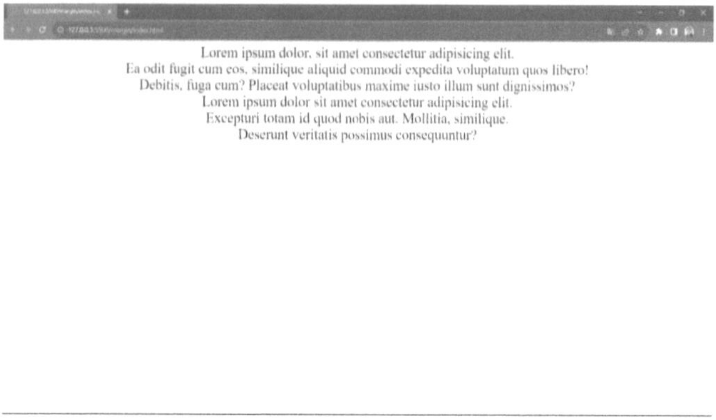

Lorem ipsum dolor, sit amet consectetur adipisicing elit.
Ea odit fugit cum eos, similique aliquid commodi expedita voluptatum quos libero!
Debitis, fuga cum? Placeat voluptatibus maxime iusto illum sunt dignissimos?
Lorem ipsum dolor sit amet consectetur adipisicing elit.
Excepturi totam id quod nobis aut. Mollitia, similique.
Deserunt veritatis possimus consequuntur?

```css
p {

    font-size: 30px;

    text-align: center;

}
```

```
2  p {
3      font-size: 30px;
4      text-align: center;
5  }
```

justify

Stretches the lines so that each line has equal width (like in newspapers and magazines) .
The text must extend over more than one line for justification to work. Use the text-align-last property to align the last line.

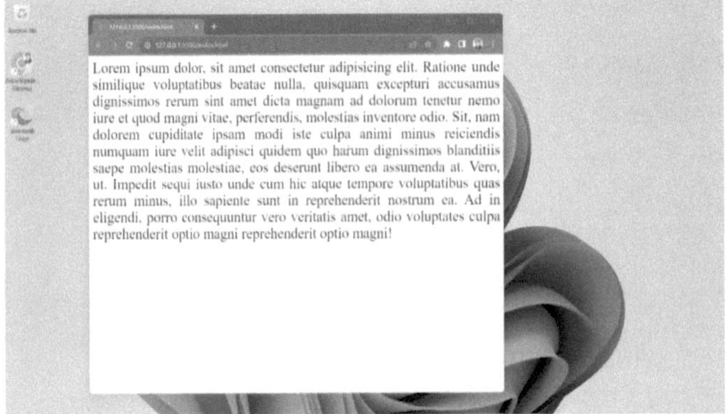

This is what it looked like before justification.

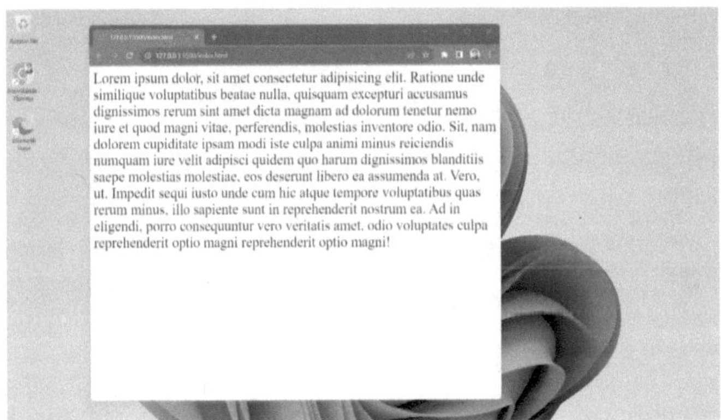

```
<style>

  p {

    font-size: 30px;

    text-align: justify;

  }

</style>

<p>
```

Lorem ipsum dolor, sit amet consectetur adipisicing elit. Ratione unde
  similique voluptatibus beatae nulla, quisquam excepturi accusamus dignissimos
  rerum sint amet dicta magnam ad dolorum tenetur nemo iure et quod magni vitae,
  perferendis, molestias inventore odio. Sit, nam dolorem cupiditate ipsam modi
  iste culpa animi minus reiciendis numquam iure velit adipisci quidem quo harum
  dignissimos blanditiis saepe molestias molestiae, eos deserunt libero ea
  assumenda at. Vero, ut. Impedit sequi iusto unde cum hic atque tempore
  voluptatibus quas rerum minus, illo sapiente sunt in reprehenderit nostrum ea.
  Ad in eligendi, porro consequuntur vero veritatis amet, odio voluptates culpa
  reprehenderit optio magni reprehenderit optio magni!
</p>

```html
<style>
  p {
    font-size: 30px;
    text-align: justify;
  }
</style>
<p>
  Lorem ipsum dolor, sit amet consectetur adipisicing elit. Ratione unde
  similique voluptatibus beatae nulla, quisquam excepturi accusamus dignissimos
  rerum sint amet dicta magnam ad dolorum tenetur nemo iure et quod magni vitae,
  perferendis, molestias inventore odio. Sit, nam dolorem cupiditate ipsam modi
  iste culpa animi minus reiciendis numquam iure velit adipisci quidem quo harum
  dignissimos blanditiis saepe molestias molestiae, eos deserunt libero ea
  assumenda at. Vero, ut. Impedit sequi iusto unde cum hic atque tempore
  voluptatibus quas rerum minus, illo sapiente sunt in reprehenderit nostrum ea.
  Ad in eligendi, porro consequuntur vero veritatis amet, odio voluptates culpa
  reprehenderit optio magni reprehenderit optio magni!
</p>
```

text-align-last

The CSS property text-align-last defines how the last line of a block or a line is aligned directly before a forced line break.

Values

- auto
- left
- right
- center
- justify
- start
- end

justify

The text is justified.

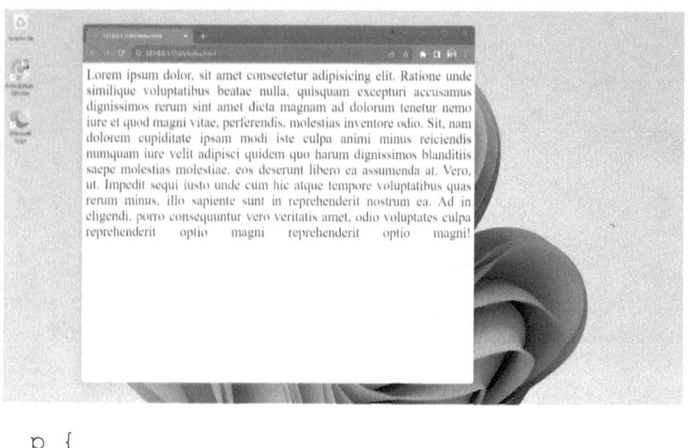

```css
p {

    font-size: 30px;

    text-align: justify;

    text-align-last: justify;

}
```

```
2  p {
3    font-size: 30px;
4    text-align: justify;
5    text-align-last: justify;
6  }
```

center

The inline contents are centered within the line box.

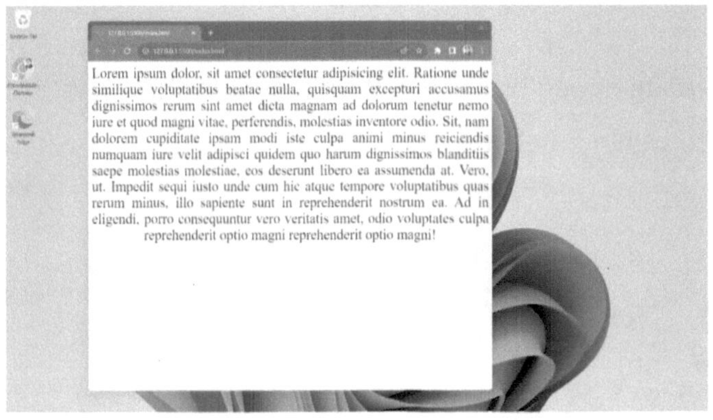

```css
p {
    font-size: 30px;
    text-align: justify;
    text-align-last: center;
}
```

start

The last line is aligned with the beginning of the line (left if the text direction is from left to right, and right if the text direction is from right to left)

end

The last line is aligned at the end of the line (right if the text direction is from left to right, and left if the text direction is from right to left)

white-space

The white-space property determines how the white space within an element is handled

- normal (default)
- nowrap
- pre
- pre-line
- pre-wrap

normal (default)

Sequences of whitespace will collapse into a single whitespace. Text will wrap when necessary.

Lorem ipsum dolor sit amet consectetur, adipisicing elit. Ipsam voluptatem consectetur esse, odio asperiores laboriosam sequi consequatur deserunt laborum aspernatur explicabo quae ab dolorem, itaque soluta adipisci dolores nobis placeat reiciendis a vel, corrupti exercitationem tempore. Dicta cum error nam quis illum asperiores? Quis perspiciatis perferendis totam maiores eveniet non provident, dolore tenetur dignissimos cum modi. Eveniet commodi, fugit sequi sed non quos nobis expedita incidunt animi eos cumque corrupti quod corporis mollitia provident laboriosam accusantium omnis ducimus, esse culpa. Labore excepturi incidunt saepe reprehenderit libero autem unde suscipit repellat, sapiente esse dolorem eius eaque provident doloribus ipsa nulla odio?

```
<style>
  p {
    font-size: 30px;
    color: blue;
```

```css
      white-space: normal;
  }
</style>
<p>
  Lorem ipsum dolor sit amet consectetur,
adipisicing elit. Ipsam voluptatem
  consectetur esse, odio asperiores laboriosam
sequi consequatur deserunt
  laborum aspernatur explicabo quae ab dolorem,
itaque soluta adipisci dolores
  nobis placeat reiciendis a vel, corrupti
exercitationem tempore. Dicta cum
  error nam quis illum asperiores? Quis
perspiciatis perferendis totam maiores
  eveniet non provident, dolore tenetur
dignissimos eum modi. Eveniet commodi,
  fugit sequi sed non quos nobis expedita
incidunt animi eos cumque corrupti
  quod corporis mollitia provident laboriosam
accusantium omnis ducimus, esse
  culpa. <br />Labore excepturi incidunt saepe
reprehenderit libero autem unde
  suscipit repellat, sapiente esse dolorem eius
eaque provident doloribus ipsa
  nulla odio?
</p>
```

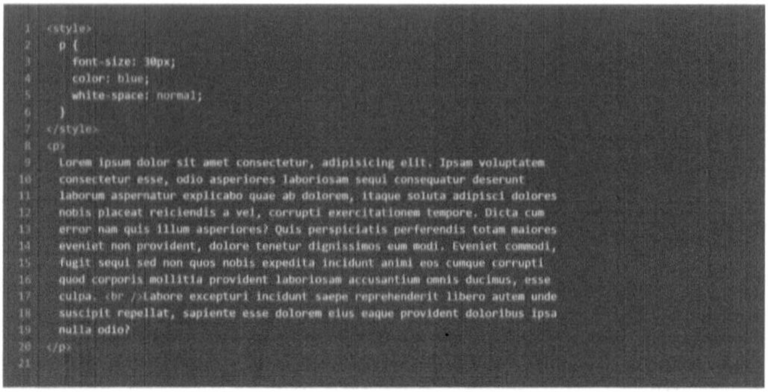

```html
<style>
  p {
    font-size: 30px;
    color: blue;
    white-space: normal;
  }
</style>
<p>
  Lorem ipsum dolor sit amet consectetur, adipisicing elit. Ipsam voluptatem
  consectetur esse, odio asperiores laboriosam sequi consequatur deserunt
  laborum aspernatur explicabo quae ab dolorem, itaque soluta adipisci dolores
  nobis placeat reiciendis a vel, corrupti exercitationem tempore. Dicta cum
  error nam quis illum asperiores? Quis perspiciatis perferendis totam maiores
  eveniet non provident, dolore tenetur dignissimos eum modi. Eveniet commodi,
  fugit sequi sed non quos nobis expedita incidunt animi eos cumque corrupti
  quod corporis mollitia provident laboriosam accusantium omnis ducimus, esse
  culpa. <br />Labore excepturi incidunt saepe reprehenderit libero autem unde
  suscipit repellat, sapiente esse dolorem eius eaque provident doloribus ipsa
  nulla odio?
</p>
```

nowrap

Sequences of spaces are combined into a single space.

The text never breaks into the next line. The text

continues on the same line until a tag appears

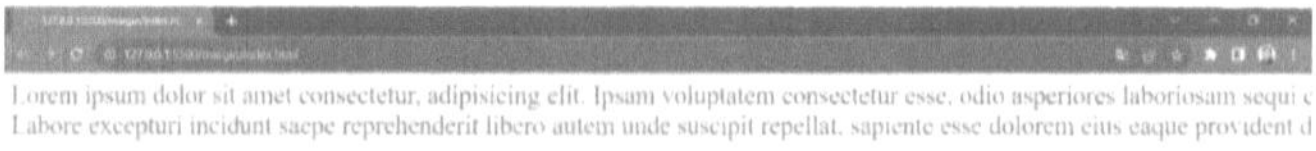

```css
p {
    font-size: 30px;
    color: blue;
    white-space: nowrap;
}
```

```css
p {
  font-size: 30px;
  color: blue;
  white-space: nowrap;
}
```

pre

The whitespace is retained by the browser. The text is only wrapped at line breaks. Behaves like the tag in HTML

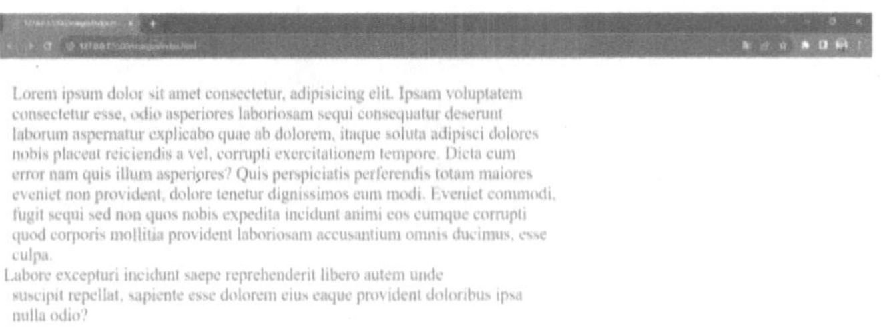

```css
p {
  font-size: 30px;
  color: blue;
  white-space: pre;
}
```

pre-line

Sequences of whitespace will collapse into a single whitespace. Text will wrap when necessary, and on line breaks

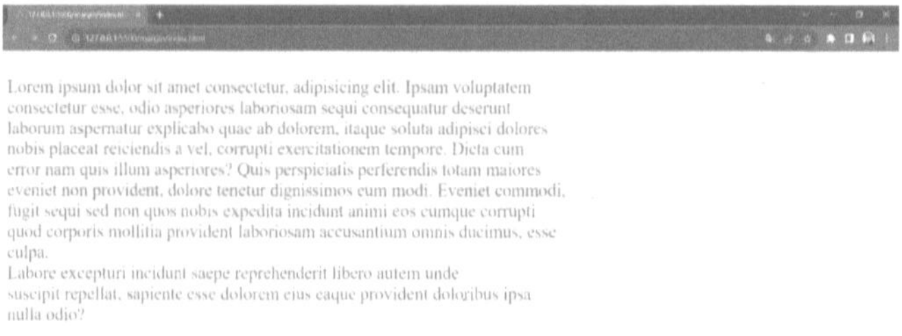

```
p {
    font-size: 30px;
    color: blue;
    white-space: pre-line;
}
```

pre-wrap

The whitespace is retained by the browser. Text is wrapped if necessary, and for line breaks

Lorem ipsum dolor sit amet consectetur, adipisicing elit. Ipsam voluptatem consectetur esse, odio asperiores laboriosam sequi consequatur deserunt laborum aspernatur explicabo quae ab dolorem, itaque soluta adipisci dolores nobis placeat reiciendis a vel, corrupti exercitationem tempore. Dicta cum error nam quis illum asperiores? Quis perspiciatis perferendis totam maiores eveniet non provident, dolore tenetur dignissimos eum modi. Eveniet commodi, fugit sequi sed non quos nobis expedita incidunt animi eos cumque corrupti quod corporis mollitia provident laboriosam accusantium omnis ducimus, esse culpa.
Labore excepturi incidunt saepe reprehenderit libero autem unde suscipit repellat, sapiente esse dolorem eius eaque provident doloribus ipsa nulla odio?

```css
p {
    font-size: 30px;
    color: blue;
    white-space: pre-wrap;
}
```

writing-mode

The writing-mode property specifies whether lines of text are laid out horizontally or vertically.

Values

- horizontal-tb
- vertical-rl
- vertical-lr

Content flows horizontally from left to right, vertically from top to bottom.

Lorem ipsum dolor sit amet consectetur, adipisicing elit. Laudantium, unde.

```
<style>
  .wrapper {
    width: 100%;
    font-size: 30px;
    writing-mode: horizontal-tb;
  }
</style>
<div class="wrapper">
  Lorem ipsum dolor sit amet consectetur,
adipisicing elit. Laudantium, unde.
</div>
```

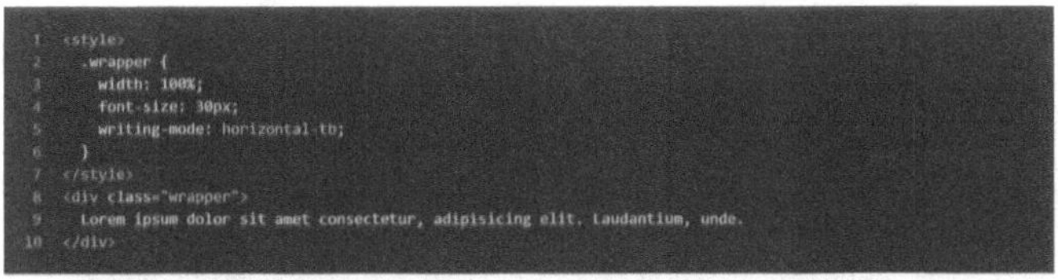

```html
<style>
  .wrapper {
    width: 100%;
    font-size: 30px;
    writing-mode: horizontal-tb;
  }
</style>
<div class="wrapper">
  Lorem ipsum dolor sit amet consectetur, adipisicing elit. Laudantium, unde.
</div>
```

vertical-rl

Content flows vertically from top to bottom, horizontally from right to left.

```html
<style>
  .wrapper {
    width: 100%;
    font-size: 30px;
    writing-mode: vertical-lr;
  }
</style>
<div class="wrapper">
  Lorem ipsum dolor sit amet consectetur,
adipisicing elit. Laudantium, unde.
```

```
</div>
```

```
1  <style>
2    .wrapper {
3      width: 100%;
4      font-size: 30px;
5      writing-mode: vertical-lr;
6    }
7  </style>
8  <div class="wrapper">
9    lorem ipsum dolor sit amet consectetur, adipisicing elit. Laudantium, unde.
10 </div>
```

vertical-lr

Content flows vertically from top to bottom, horizontally from left to right.

```
<style>
  .wrapper {
    width: 100%;
    font-size: 30px;
    writing-mode: vertical-rl;
  }
</style>
<div class="wrapper">
```

Lorem ipsum dolor sit amet consectetur,
adipisicing elit. Laudantium, unde.
</div>

```
1   <style>
2     .wrapper {
3       width: 100%;
4       font-size: 30px;
5       writing-mode: vertical-rl;
6     }
7   </style>
8   <div class="wrapper">
9     Lorem ipsum dolor sit amet consectetur, adipisicing elit. Laudantium, unde.
10  </div>
```

Chapter 3: Typography properties

word-break

The word-break property determines how words are to be broken when they reach the end of a line.

Values

- normal (default)
- break-all
- keep-all

normal (default)

Uses default line break rules.

Lorem ipsum, dolor sit amet consectetur adipisicing elit. Esse asperiores voluptatum obcaecati mollitia veryveryverylonglongwordword possimus rerum itaque? Incidunt, culpa dolorem necessitatibus officiis tempore modi! Odit minima reprehenderit voluptatibus provident.
Consequuntur officiis magnam facere iure molestias. Blanditiis velit magnam explicabo consectetur odit, reprehenderitreprehenderit amet aliquid quisquam?
Labore explicabo et assumenda expedita alias ullam corporis, ducimus nulla voluptatem consequatur enim, expeditaexpeditaexpedita maiores! Minima atque quo at nam soluta vel dicta non, accusamus blanditiis nisi unde, culpa dolorem magni asperiores amet repudiandae saepe sed dolore consequuntur assumenda harum ipsum quia!
Iure, maiores quo laudantium perspiciatis corporis sint eveniet odio saepe corrupti soluta fugiat consequatur.
Lorem ipsum dolor sit amet consectetur adipisicing elit.
Nihil veniam vero consequatur rerum voluptatum corporis vitae rem provident voluptatem sed quae atque ea, explicaboexplicaboexplicabo doloribus qui, quod exercitationem expedita sint!

```html
<style>
  p {
    font-size: 30px;
```

```css
  color: blue;
  word-break: normal;
  }
  span {
  color: red;
  }
</style>
<p>
  Lorem ipsum, dolor sit amet consectetur
adipisicing elit. Esse asperiores
  voluptatum obcaecati mollitia
  <span>veryveryverylong-longwordword</span>
possimus rerum itaque? Incidunt,
  culpa dolorem necessitatibus officiis tempore
modi! Odit minima reprehenderit
  voluptatibus provident.
  <br />
Consequuntur officiis magnam facere iure
molestias. Blanditiis velit magnam
  explicabo consectetur odit,
<span>reprehenderit-reprehenderit</span> amet
  aliquid quisquam?
  <br />
Labore explicabo et assumenda expedita alias
ullam corporis, ducimus nulla
```

voluptatem consequatur enim,
<span>expedita-expeditaexpedita</span> maiores!
Minima atque quo at nam soluta vel dicta non,
accusamus blanditiis nisi unde,
culpa dolorem magni asperiores amet
repudiandae saepe sed dolore consequuntur
assumenda harum ipsum quia!

Iure, maiores quo laudantium perspiciatis
corporis sint eveniet odio saepe
corrupti soluta fugiat consequatur.

Lorem ipsum dolor sit amet consectetur
adipisicing elit.

Nihil veniam vero consequatur rerum
voluptatum corporis vitae rem provident
voluptatem sed quae atque ea,
<span>explicaboexplicaboexplicabo</span>
doloribus qui, quod exercitationem
expedita sint!
</p>

```html
<style>
  p {
    font-size: 30px;
    color: blue;
    word-break: normal;
  }
  span {
    color: red;
  }
</style>
<p>
  Lorem ipsum, dolor sit amet consectetur adipisicing elit. Esse asperiores
  voluptatum obcaecati mollitia
  <span>veryveryverylong-longwordword</span> possimus rerum itaque? Incidunt,
  culpa dolorem necessitatibus officiis tempore modi! Odit minima reprehenderit
  voluptatibus provident.
  <br />
  Consequuntur officiis magnam facere iure molestias. Blanditiis velit magnam
  explicabo consectetur odit, <span>reprehenderit-reprehenderit</span> amet
  aliquid quisquam?
  <br />
  Labore explicabo et assumenda expedita alias ullam corporis, ducimus nulla
  voluptatem consequatur enim, <span>expedita-expeditaexpedita</span> maiores!
  Minima atque quo at nam soluta vel dicta non, accusamus blanditiis nisi unde,
  culpa dolorem magni asperiores amet repudiandae saepe sed dolore consequuntur
  assumenda harum ipsum quia!
  <br />
  Iure, maiores quo laudantium perspiciatis corporis sint eveniet odio saepe
  corrupti soluta fugiat consequatur.
  <br />
  Lorem ipsum dolor sit amet consectetur adipisicing elit.
  <br />
  Nihil veniam vero consequatur rerum voluptatum corporis vitae rem provident
  voluptatem sed quae atque ea,
  <span>explicaboexplicaboexplicabo</span> doloribus qui, quod exercitationem
  expedita sint!
</p>
```

break-all

To prevent overflow, word may be broken at any character

p {

```css
    font-size: 30px;

    color: blue;

    word-break: break-all;

}
```

```
2  p {
3    font-size: 30px;
4    color: blue;
5    word-break: break-all;
6  }
```

keep-all

Word breaks should not be used for Chinese/Japanese/Korean (CJK) text. Non-CJK text behaves in the same way as the "normal" value

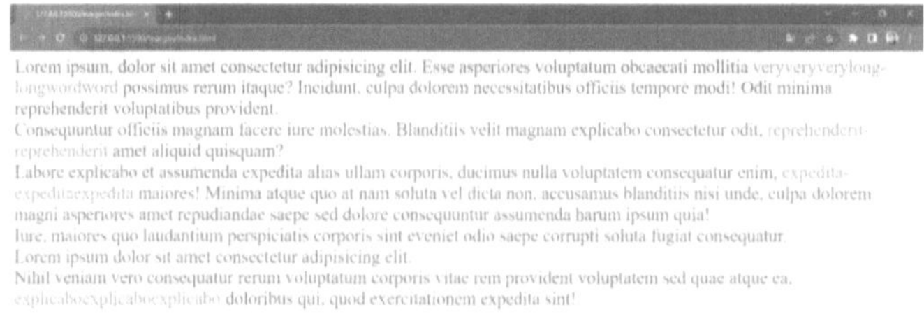

```css
p {

    font-size: 30px;

    color: blue;

    word-break: keep-all;

}
```

```css
p {
  font-size: 30px;
  color: blue;
  word-break: keep-all;
}
```

text-rendering

The CSS property text-rendering gives the rendering engine information about what it should optimize for when rendering text.

The browser makes trade-offs between speed, readability and geometric precision.

Values

- optimizeSpeed
- optimizeLegibility

optimizeSpeed

When drawing text, the browser places more value on speed than on legibility and geometric precision. It deactivates kerning and ligatures.

file flair

```
<style>
  @import
url(http://fonts.googleapis.com/css?family=Lato
:400,400italic,700italic,900italic);
  p {
    font-size: 200px;
    color: blue;
    text-indent: 100px;
    font-family: "Lato", sans-serif;
    text-rendering: optimizeSpeed;
  }
</style>
<p>file flair</p>
```

```
 1  <style>
 2    @import url(http://fonts.googleapis.com/css?family=Lato:400,400italic,700italic,900italic);
 3    p {
 4      font-size: 200px;
 5      color: blue;
 6      text-indent: 100px;
 7      font-family: "Lato", sans-serif;
 8      text-rendering: optimizeSpeed;
 9    }
10  </style>
11  <p>file flair</p>
```

optimizeLegibility

The browser prioritizes readability over display speed and geometric precision. This enables kerning and optional ligatures.

```
p {
    font-size: 200px;
    color: blue;
    text-indent: 100px;
    font-family: "Lato", sans-serif;
    text-rendering: optimizeLegibility;
}
```

```css
3  p {
4      font-size: 200px;
5      color: blue;
6      text-indent: 100px;
7      font-family: "Lato", sans-serif;
8      text-rendering: optimizeLegibility;
9  }
```

Kerning and ligatures

Kerning and ligatures are typographic concepts related to the spacing and arrangement of characters in a text.

Kerning

Kerning refers to the adjustment of the spacing between pairs of characters. It is used to achieve visually pleasing and balanced spacing between specific character combinations. Kerning is particularly important for improving the readability and aesthetics of headlines, logos, and display text. In CSS, you can control kerning using the letter-spacing property.

Ligatures

Ligatures are special characters that combine two or more individual characters into a single typographic glyph. They are used to improve the readability and appearance of certain character combinations. Ligatures are commonly found in scripts like cursive or calligraphy fonts. For example, in some fonts, the combination of the letters "f" and "i" may be replaced with a ligature that joins the two letters together. In CSS, you can enable or disable ligatures using the font-variant-ligatures property.

It's worth noting that not all fonts support kerning and ligatures, and the availability and behavior of these features can vary depending on the font and the browser being used to render the text.

Chapter 4: Visual effects properties

text-shadow

The CSS property text-shadow adds shadows to the text. It accepts a comma-separated list of shadows to be applied to the text and its decorations. Each shadow is described by a combination of X and Y offset to the element, blur radius and color.

Values

- none (default)
- offset-x(Required) offset-y(Required) blur-radius color

none (default)

No shadow

```
<style>
  p {
    font-size: 30px;
    color: blue;
    padding: 40px 80px;
    text-shadow: none;
  }
</style>
<p>
  Lorem ipsum dolor sit amet consectetur
adipisicing elit. Aspernatur rem quae
  soluta nam aliquid assumenda dolorum.
Dignissimos incidunt beatae illo
  adipisci vitae exercitationem ad, dicta,
quasi optio suscipit minima autem
  reprehenderit provident? Ducimus quod
doloribus eligendi vero id mollitia
  animi repudiandae reiciendis voluptate? Non
minima, id dignissimos at ipsum
  quidem.
</p>
```

```
1  <style>
2    p {
3      font-size: 30px;
4      color: blue;
5      padding: 40px 80px;
6      text-shadow: none;
7    }
8  </style>
9  <p>
10   Lorem ipsum dolor sit amet consectetur adipisicing elit. Aspernatur rem quae
11   soluta nam aliquid assumenda dolorum. Dignissimos incidunt beatae illo
12   adipisci vitae exercitationem ad, dicta, quasi optio suscipit minima autem
13   reprehenderit provident? Ducimus quod doloribus eligendi vero id mollitia
14   animi repudiandae reiciendis voluptate? Non minima, id dignissimos at ipsum
15   quidem.
16  </p>
```

offset-x offset-y blur-radius color

Lorem ipsum dolor sit amet consectetur adipisicing elit. Aspernatur rem quae soluta nam aliquid assumenda dolorum. Dignissimos incidunt beatae illo adipisci vitae exercitationem ad, dicta, quasi optio suscipit minima autem reprehenderit provident? Ducimus quod doloribus eligendi vero id mollitia animi repudiandae reiciendis voluptate? Non minima, id dignissimos at ipsum quidem.

```
p {
    font-size: 30px;
    color: blue;
    padding: 40px 80px;
    text-shadow: 5px 5px 5px rgba(255, 0, 255, 0.5);
}
```

```
2  p {
3    font-size: 30px;
4    color: blue;
5    padding: 40px 80px;
6    text-shadow: 5px 5px 5px rgba(255, 0, 255, 0.5);
7  }
```

color

The color property specifies the color of text.

Values

- color

See *Chapter 3: Values and Units* to know which color values you can use.

color

Specifies the text color

```
p {
    font-size: 30px;
    padding: 100px;
    color: blue;
}
```

```css
p {
    font-size: 30px;
    padding: 100px;
    color: blue;
}
```

vertical-align

The vertical-align CSS property sets the vertical alignment of an inline or inline-block.

Values

- baseline (default)
- length
- %
- sub
- super
- top
- text-top
- middle
- bottom
- text-bottom

baseline (default)

The element is aligned with the baseline of the parent.

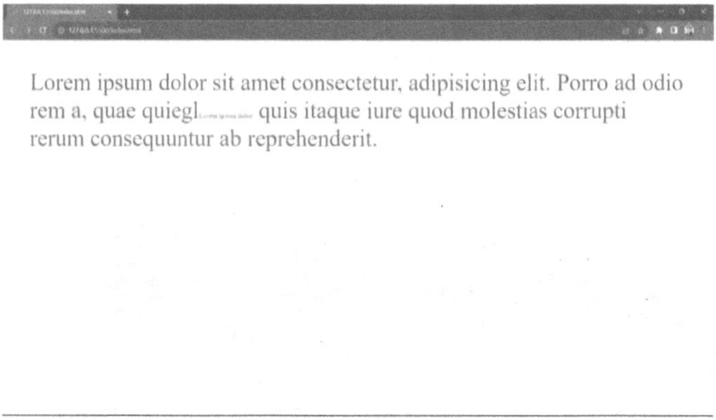

Lorem ipsum dolor sit amet consectetur, adipisicing elit. Porro ad odio rem a, quae quiegl........... quis itaque iure quod molestias corrupti rerum consequuntur ab reprehenderit.

```
<style>
  p {
    font-size: 50px;
    padding: 50px;
    color: blue;
  }
  span {
    font-size: 14px;
    font-weight: bold;
    color: red;
    vertical-align: baseline;
  }
</style>
<p>
  Lorem ipsum dolor sit amet consectetur,
adipisicing elit. Porro ad odio rem a,
```

```
    quae quiegl<span>Lorem ipsum dolor</span>
quis itaque iure quod molestias
    corrupti rerum consequuntur ab reprehenderit.
</p>
```

```
1   <style>
2     p {
3       font-size: 50px;
4       padding: 50px;
5       color: blue;
6     }
7     span {
8       font-size: 14px;
9       font-weight: bold;
10      color: red;
11      vertical-align: baseline;
12    }
13  </style>
14  <p>
15    Lorem ipsum dolor sit amet consectetur, adipisicing elit. Porro ad odio rem a,
16    quae quiegl<span>Lorem ipsum dolor</span> quis itaque iure quod molestias
17    corrupti rerum consequuntur ab reprehenderit.
18  </p>
```

length

Raises or lowers an element by the specified length. Negative values are allowed.

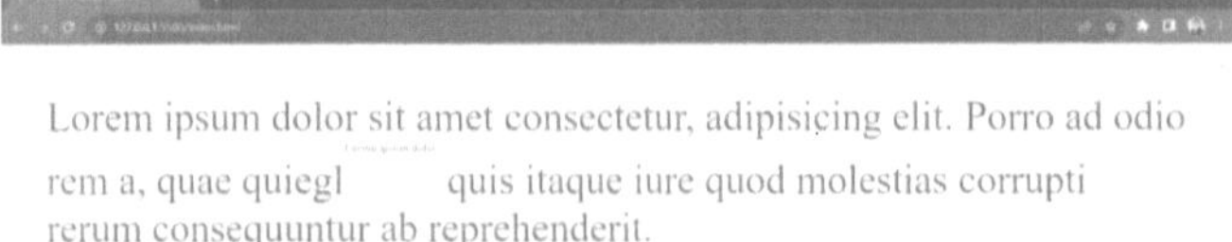


```
span {
    font-size: 14px;
```

```css
    font-weight: bold;
    color: red;
    vertical-align: 50px;
}
```

```css
7   span {
8       font-size: 14px;
9       font-weight: bold;
10      color: red;
11      vertical-align: 50px;
12  }
```

negative length

Lorem ipsum dolor sit amet consectetur, adipisicing elit. Porro ad odio
rem a, quae quiegl   quis itaque iure quod molestias corrupti

rerum consequuntur ab reprehenderit.

```css
span {
    font-size: 14px;
    font-weight: bold;
    color: red;
    vertical-align: -50px;
}
```

```
 7   span {
 8     font-size: 14px;
 9     font-weight: bold;
10     color: red;
11     vertical-align: -50px;
12   }
```

%

Increases or decreases an element by a percentage value of the line-height property. Negative values are permitted.

Lorem ipsum dolor sit amet consectetur, adipisicing elit. Porro ad odio rem a, quae quiegl——————— quis itaque iure quod molestias corrupti rerum consequuntur ab reprehenderit.

```
span {
    font-size: 14px;
    font-weight: bold;
    color: red;
    vertical-align: 50%;
}
```

```
 6   span {
 7     font-size: 20px;
 8     font-weight: bold;
 9     color: red;
10     vertical-align: 130%;
11   }
```

negative %

Lorem ipsum dolor sit amet consectetur, adipisicing elit. Porro ad odio rem a, quae quiegl_________ quis itaque iure quod molestias corrupti rerum consequuntur ab reprehenderit.

```css
span {
    font-size: 14px;
    font-weight: bold;
    color: red;
    vertical-align: -50%;
}
```

```
 7   span {
 8      font-size: 14px;
 9      font-weight: bold;
10      color: red;
11      vertical-align: -50%;
12   }
```

sub

The element is aligned with the subscript baseline of the parent

Lorem ipsum dolor sit amet consectetur, adipisicing elit. Porro ad odio rem a, quae quiegl______ quis itaque iure quod molestias corrupti rerum consequuntur ab reprehenderit.

```css
span {
    font-size: 14px;
    font-weight: bold;
    color: red;
    vertical-align: sub;
}
```

```
 7  span {
 8      font-size: 14px;
 9      font-weight: bold;
10      color: red;
11      vertical-align: sub;
12  }
```

super

The element is aligned with the superscript baseline of the parent

Lorem ipsum dolor sit amet consectetur, adipisicing elit. Porro ad odio rem a, quae quiegl quis itaque iure quod molestias corrupti rerum consequuntur ab reprehenderit.

```css
span {
    font-size: 14px;
    font-weight: bold;
    color: red;
    vertical-align: super;
}
```

```css
 7  span {
 8      font-size: 14px;
 9      font-weight: bold;
10      color: red;
11      vertical-align: super;
12  }
```

top

The element is aligned with the top of the tallest element on the line

Lorem ipsum dolor sit amet consectetur, adipisicing elit. Porro ad odio rem a, quae quiegl quis itaque iure quod molestias corrupti rerum consequuntur ab reprehenderit.

```css
span {
    font-size: 14px;
    font-weight: bold;
    color: red;
    vertical-align: top;
}
```

```css
 7  span {
 8      font-size: 14px;
 9      font-weight: bold;
10      color: red;
11      vertical-align: top;
12  }
```

text-top

The element is aligned with the top of the parent element's font

Lorem ipsum dolor sit amet consectetur, adipisicing elit. Porro ad odio rem a, quae quiegl quis itaque iure quod molestias corrupti rerum consequuntur ab reprehenderit.

```css
span {
    font-size: 14px;
    font-weight: bold;
    color: red;
    vertical-align: text-top;
}
```

```css
7  span {
8      font-size: 14px;
9      font-weight: bold;
10     color: red;
11     vertical-align: text-top;
12 }
```

middle

The element is placed in the middle of the parent element

Lorem ipsum dolor sit amet consectetur, adipisicing elit. Porro ad odio rem a, quae quiegl———— quis itaque iure quod molestias corrupti rerum consequuntur ab reprehenderit.

```css
span {

    font-size: 14px;

    font-weight: bold;

    color: red;

    vertical-align: middle;

}
```

```css
 7  span {
 8      font-size: 14px;
 9      font-weight: bold;
10      color: red;
11      vertical-align: middle;
12  }
```

bottom

The element is aligned with the lowest element on the line

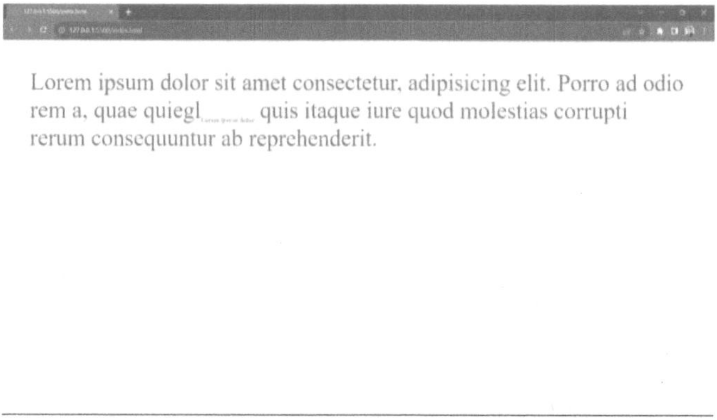

Lorem ipsum dolor sit amet consectetur, adipisicing elit. Porro ad odio rem a, quae quiegl............ quis itaque iure quod molestias corrupti rerum consequuntur ab reprehenderit.

```css
span {
    font-size: 14px;
    font-weight: bold;
    color: red;
    vertical-align: bottom;
}
```

```css
7  span {
8      font-size: 14px;
9      font-weight: bold;
10     color: red;
11     vertical-align: bottom;
12  }
```

text-bottom

The element is aligned with the bottom of the parent element's font

Lorem ipsum dolor sit amet consectetur, adipisicing elit. Porro ad odio
rem a, quae quiegl............ quis itaque iure quod molestias corrupti
rerum consequuntur ab reprehenderit.

```css
span {
    font-size: 14px;
    font-weight: bold;
    color: red;
    vertical-align: text-bottom;
}
```

```css
7  span {
8      font-size: 14px;
9      font-weight: bold;
10     color: red;
11     vertical-align: text-bottom;
12 }
```

text-overflow

The text-overflow property defines how overflowed
content that is not displayed should be signaled to the
user. It can be truncated, display an ellipsis (...) or
display a user-defined character string.

The text-overflow property does not force an overflow. In
order for the text to overflow its container, you must set

other CSS properties: Overflow and whitespace. For example:

```
overflow: hidden;
white-space: nowrap;
```


- clip (default)
- ellipsis
- string (experimental)

The text is clipped and not accessible

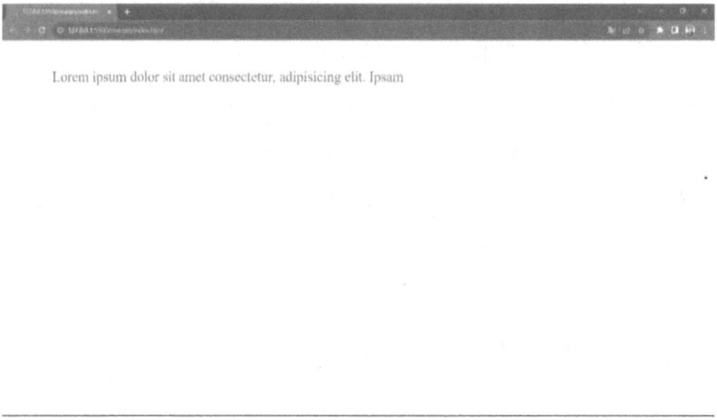

Lorem ipsum dolor sit amet consectetur, adipisicing elit. Ipsam

---

```
<style>
  p {
    margin-top: 60px;
    margin-left: 100px;
    width: 50%;
    font-size: 30px;
```

```
    color: blue;
    overflow: hidden;
    white-space: nowrap;
    text-overflow: clip;
  }
</style>
<p>
```

Lorem ipsum dolor sit amet consectetur,
adipisicing elit. Ipsam voluptatem
consectetur esse, odio asperiores laboriosam
sequi consequatur deserunt
laborum aspernatur explicabo quae ab dolorem,
itaque soluta adipisci dolores
nobis placeat reiciendis a vel, corrupti
exercitationem tempore. Dicta cum
error nam quis illum asperiores? Quis
perspiciatis perferendis totam maiores
eveniet non provident, dolore tenetur
dignissimos eum modi. Eveniet commodi,
fugit sequi sed non quos nobis expedita
incidunt animi eos cumque corrupti
quod corporis mollitia provident laboriosam
accusantium omnis ducimus, esse
culpa. Labore excepturi incidunt saepe
reprehenderit libero autem unde

suscipit repellat, sapiente esse dolorem eius
eaque provident doloribus ipsa
    nulla odio?
</p>

```html
1   <style>
2     p {
3       margin-top: 60px;
4       margin-left: 100px;
5       width: 50%;
6       font-size: 30px;
7       color: blue;
8       overflow: hidden;
9       white-space: nowrap;
10      text-overflow: clip;
11    }
12  </style>
13  <p>
14    Lorem ipsum dolor sit amet consectetur, adipisicing elit. Ipsam voluptatem
15    consectetur esse, odio asperiores laboriosam sequi consequatur deserunt
16    laborum aspernatur explicabo quae ab dolorem, itaque soluta adipisci dolores
17    nobis placeat reiciendis a vel, corrupti exercitationem tempore. Dicta cum
18    error nam quis illum asperiores? Quis perspiciatis perferendis totam maiores
19    eveniet non provident, dolore tenetur dignissimos eum modi. Eveniet commodi,
20    fugit sequi sed non quos nobis expedita incidunt animi eos cumque corrupti
21    quod corporis mollitia provident laboriosam accusantium omnis ducimus, esse
22    culpa. Labore excepturi incidunt saepe reprehenderit libero autem unde
23    suscipit repellat, sapiente esse dolorem eius eaque provident doloribus ipsa
24    nulla odio?
25  </p>
26
```

ellipsis

Render an ellipsis ("...") to represent the clipped text

```
p {
    margin-top: 60px;
```

```
    margin-left: 100px;
    width: 50%;
    font-size: 30px;
    color: blue;
    overflow: hidden;
    white-space: nowrap;
    text-overflow: ellipsis;
}
```

```
 2  p {
 3      margin-top: 60px;
 4      margin-left: 100px;
 5      width: 50%;
 6      font-size: 30px;
 7      color: blue;
 8      overflow: hidden;
 9      white-space: nowrap;
10      text-overflow: ellipsis;
11  }
```

Chapter 5: Text styling properties

text-decoration

The text-decoration property specifies the decoration added to text, and is a shorthand property

text-decoration: <text-decoration-style> <text-decoration-line (required)> <text-decoration-color> <text-decoration-thickness>

Values

- text-decoration-style

    text-decoration-line(required)

    text-decoration-color text-decoration-thickness

text-decoration-style

- solid
- double
- dotted
- dashed
- wavy

text-decoration-line

- none

- underline
- overline
- line-through

text-decoration-color

- color

text-decoration-thickness

- auto
- from-font
- length
- %

wavy underline red 3px

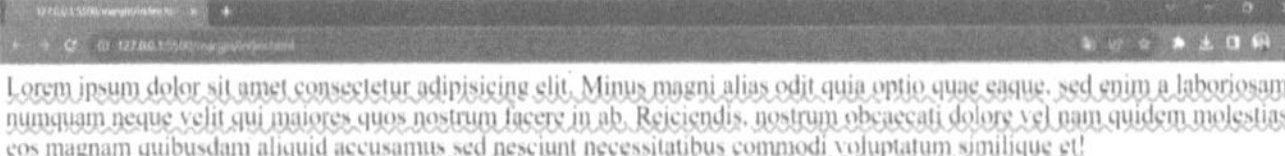

```
<style>
  p {
    font-size: 30px;
    text-decoration: wavy underline red 3px;
```

```
    }
</style>
<p>
    Lorem ipsum dolor sit amet consectetur
adipisicing elit. Minus magni alias
    odit quia optio quae eaque, sed enim a
laboriosam numquam neque velit qui
    maiores quos nostrum facere in ab.
Reiciendis, nostrum obcaecati dolore vel
    nam quidem molestias eos magnam quibusdam
aliquid accusamus sed nesciunt
    necessitatibus commodi voluptatum similique
et!
</p>
```

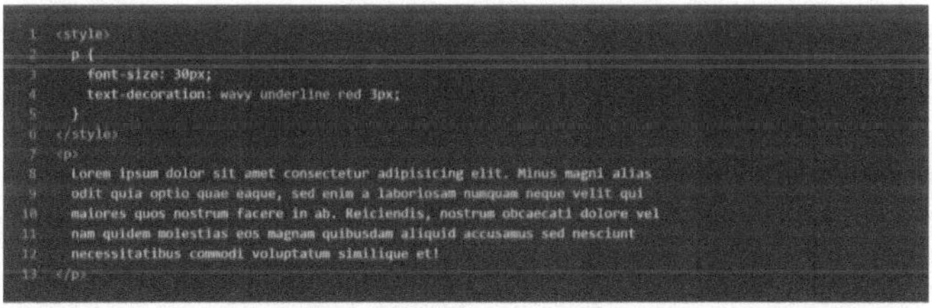

```
1   <style>
2     p {
3       font-size: 30px;
4       text-decoration: wavy underline red 3px;
5     }
6   </style>
7   <p>
8     Lorem ipsum dolor sit amet consectetur adipisicing elit. Minus magni alias
9     odit quia optio quae eaque, sed enim a laboriosam numquam neque velit qui
10    maiores quos nostrum facere in ab. Reiciendis, nostrum obcaecati dolore vel
11    nam quidem molestias eos magnam quibusdam aliquid accusamus sed nesciunt
12    necessitatibus commodi voluptatum similique et!
13  </p>
```

dashed overline fuchsia 3px

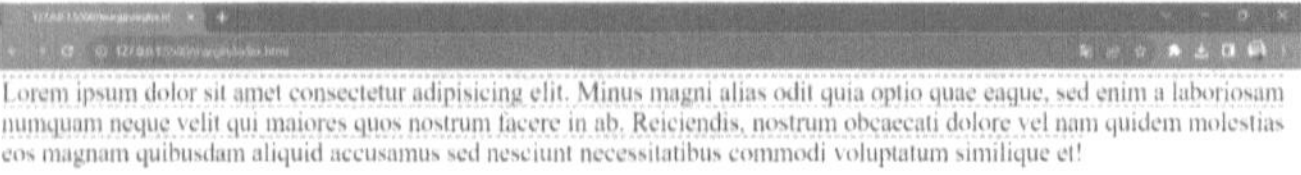

```css
p {
    font-size: 30px;
    text-decoration: dashed overline fuchsia 3px;
}
```

letter-spacing

The letter-spacing property increases or decreases the space between characters in a text.

Values

- normal
- length

normal

Lorem ipsum dolor sit amet consectetur adipisicing elit. Minus magni alias odit quia optio quae eaque, sed enim a laboriosam numquam neque velit qui maiores quos nostrum facere in ab. Reiciendis, nostrum obcaecati dolore vel nam quidem molestias eos magnam quibusdam aliquid accusamus sed nesciunt necessitatibus commodi voluptatum similique et!

```css
p {

    font-size: 30px;

    letter-spacing: normal;

}
```

length

Lorem ipsum dolor sit amet consectetur adipisicing elit. Minus magni alias odit quia optio quae eaque, sed enim a laboriosam numquam neque velit qui maiores quos nostrum facere in ab. Reiciendis, nostrum obcaecati dolore vel nam quidem molestias eos magnam quibusdam aliquid accusamus sed nesciunt necessitatibus commodi voluptatum similique et!

```css
p {
    font-size: 30px;
    letter-spacing: 6px;
}
```

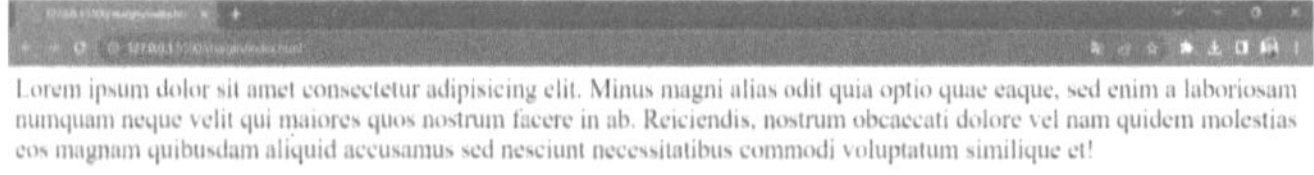

word-spacing

The word-spacing property increases or decreases the white space between words.

Values

- normal (default)
- length

normal (default)

Defines normal space between words (0.25em).

```css
p {
```

```
    font-size: 30px;
    word-spacing: normal;
}
```

length

Specifies an additional space between the words (in px, pt, cm, em, etc.). Negative values are allowed.

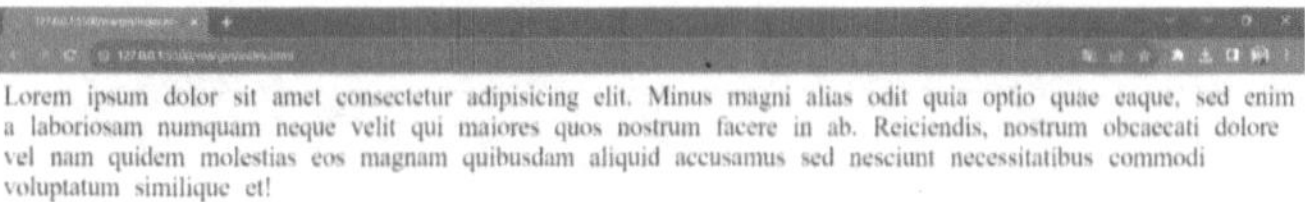


```
p {
    font-size: 30px;
    word-spacing: 10px;
}
```

negative value

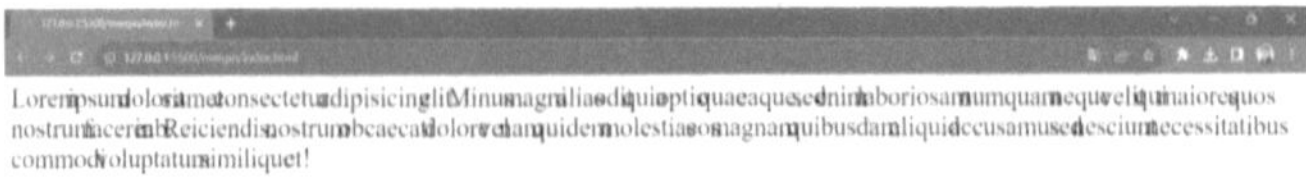

```css
p {

    font-size: 30px;

    word-spacing: -20px;

}
```

text-transform

The text-transform property controls the capitalization of text.

Values

- none (default)
- capitalize
- uppercase
- lowercase

none (default)

No capitalization. The text renders as it is.

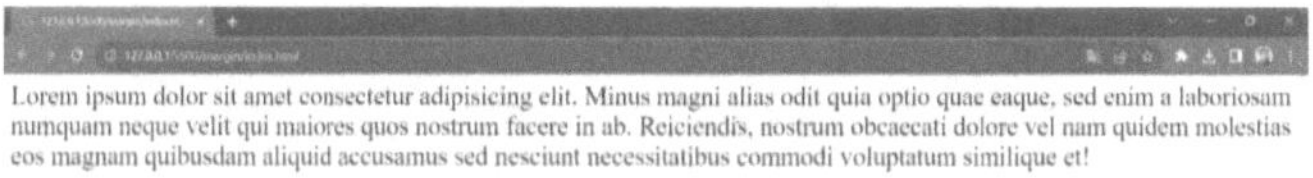

Lorem ipsum dolor sit amet consectetur adipisicing elit. Minus magni alias odit quia optio quae eaque, sed enim a laboriosam numquam neque velit qui maiores quos nostrum facere in ab. Reiciendis, nostrum obcaecati dolore vel nam quidem molestias eos magnam quibusdam aliquid accusamus sed nesciunt necessitatibus commodi voluptatum similique et!

```css
p {

    font-size: 30px;

    text-transform: none;

}
```

```
2  p {
3      font-size: 30px;
4      text-transform: none;
5  }
```

capitalize

Transforms the first character of each word to uppercase.

Lorem Ipsum Dolor Sit Amet Consectetur Adipisicing Elit. Minus Magni Alias Odit Quia Optio Quae Eaque. Sed Enim A Laboriosam Numquam Neque Velit Qui Maiores Quos Nostrum Facere In Ab. Reiciendis. Nostrum Obcaecati Dolore Vel Nam Quidem Molestias Eos Magnam Quibusdam Aliquid Accusamus Sed Nesciunt Necessitatibus Commodi Voluptatum Similique Et!

```css
p {
    font-size: 30px;
    text-transform: capitalize;
}
```

```
2  p {
3    font-size: 30px;
4    text-transform: capitalize;
5  }
```

uppercase

Transforms all characters to uppercase.

LOREM IPSUM DOLOR SIT AMET CONSECTETUR ADIPISICING ELIT. MINUS MAGNI ALIAS ODIT QUIA OPTIO QUAE EAQUE. SED ENIM A LABORIOSAM NUMQUAM NEQUE VELIT QUI MAIORES QUOS NOSTRUM FACERE IN AB. REICIENDIS. NOSTRUM OBCAECATI DOLORE VEL NAM QUIDEM MOLESTIAS EOS MAGNAM QUIBUSDAM ALIQUID ACCUSAMUS SED NESCIUNT NECESSITATIBUS COMMODI VOLUPTATUM SIMILIQUE ET!

```css
p {
    font-size: 30px;
    text-transform: uppercase;
}
```

```css
2  p {
3      font-size: 30px;
4      text-transform: uppercase;
5  }
```

lowercase

Transforms all characters to lowercase.

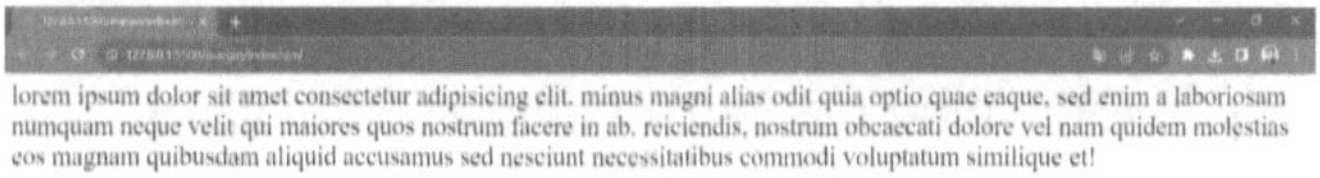

lorem ipsum dolor sit amet consectetur adipisicing elit. minus magni alias odit quia optio quae eaque. sed enim a laboriosam numquam neque velit qui maiores quos nostrum facere in ab. reiciendis. nostrum obcaecati dolore vel nam quidem molestias eos magnam quibusdam aliquid accusamus sed nesciunt necessitatibus commodi voluptatum similique et!

```css
p {
    font-size: 30px;
    text-transform: lowercase;
}
```

```css
2  p {
3      font-size: 30px;
4      text-transform: lowercase;
5  }
```

Conclusion

Congratulations! You have completed the book "CSS Typography and Web Fonts". Now you can control all aspects of web fonts and customize their properties to your needs. Remember that learning CSS is an ongoing process. Practice makes perfect — create your own projects, experiment with the features you have learned, and take advantage of the extensive online resources. Thank you for joining me in my exploration of CSS typography. I wish you the best of luck on your coding journey.

Good luck with your career and your personal brand and I will see you in other topics.

Media Attribution

Watercolor stripes background

Image by freepik

Don't miss out!

Receive an email when Abdelfattah Ragab publishes a new book. It's free and without obligation.

Also by Abdelfattah Ragab

◇ Responsive Layouts: Flex, Grid and Multi-Column

◇ Angular Portfolio App Development

◇ Stripe Integration in Angular

◇ Angular for Kids

◇ Angular for Beginners

About the Author

Abdelfattah Ragab is a professional software developer with more than 20 years of experience.
https://abdelfattah-ragab.com

About the Publisher

Abdelfattah Ragab is a highly qualified and experienced software developer with over 20 years of experience in the industry. Specializing in front-end development, Abdelfattah Ragab has a deep understanding of Angular, JavaScript, TypeScript, HTML and CSS.
Read more at https://abdelfattah-ragab.com